JASMINE MOVES IN

R J Whittaker

Also by R J Whittaker

Hannah Takes The Lead
Pom Pom The Great
Pom Pom Moves House
Pom Pom Starts School
Pom Pom The Pirate
Pom Pom the Brave
Pom Pom Helps Out

Copyright © 2013, 2021 by R J Whittaker

 Stopwatch Publications

All rights reserved. This book or any portion thereof may not be reproduced or used in any manner whatsoever without the express written permission of the publisher except for the use of brief quotations in a book review.

First edition, 2013
Second edition, 2021

ISBN: 978-1-922651-00-6

Published by R J Whittaker
www.rosemarywhittaker.com

Cover design and illustrations by Gila von Meissner for Cross The Lime.

This book is a work of fiction. Names, characters, places and incidents are the product of the author's imagination or are used fictitiously. Any resemblance to actual events, locales or persons, living or dead, is coincidental.

For Tamsin – who gave up her time to read this book and offered lots of amusing and very useful advice.

One

The whole thing starts when the *For Sale* sign is taken down and the *Sold* sign goes up. New neighbours are always fun, and I really hope they'll have children or exciting pets. I'd love a llama or boa constrictor to move into our street.

I like my pet rabbit Woffles, but he's quite boring. He wanders around the lawn, nibbling at the grass before falling asleep. I'm not allowed to bring him into the house because he leaves a little trail of raisins wherever he goes. Last Christmas, he chewed a hole in our brand-new sofa and Mum threatened to put him in a pie if I brought him inside again. So, now I have to visit him in the garden if I want to watch him nibble the grass and sleep.

A moving van arrives on Saturday morning, just as I'm leaving for my swimming lesson. By the time I get home, Mum has already taken the new neighbours a plate of cookies to welcome them to our street.

'You're in luck, Rosalie,' she says. 'Mrs Robinson seems very nice. She's just moved here from Sydney, and she has a twelve-year-old daughter who'll be going to your school. She'll probably be lonely at first, so you can help her settle in.'

'Great!' I say. 'What's her name?'

Mum smiles at my enthusiasm. 'Her name is Jasmine. She's spending the day with her aunt, but her mum says she'll be here tomorrow. You can keep an eye out for her.'

It will be great having a friend right next door. Beth will always be my best friend, but she lives half an hour away, so I can't see her whenever I feel like it.

I spend most of the following morning peering out of the window, waiting for Jasmine to arrive. Just before lunch, a shiny red car draws up next door, and a girl gets out and walks quickly up the drive. She opens her front door and disappears inside before I have time to go out and speak to her.

I run around to the back garden and stand on tiptoe to look over the fence. Jasmine is wandering around her garden, looking at the neat flowerbeds. She's taller than I am, with long, blonde hair. She's also very smartly dressed, whereas I spend most of my school holidays in shorts and old T-shirts. I feel a sudden urge to go inside and change into smarter clothes, but I tell myself not to be stupid. She won't care what I look like.

'Hi, I'm Rosalie!' I call, but Jasmine doesn't seem to hear me.

'Cooee!' I call and immediately feel even more ridiculous. Who on earth says *Cooee*?

Jasmine turns at last, giving me a half-smile. 'Yes?'

'I'm Rosalie,' I say again.

'And?' she asks.

I'm not quite sure how to answer this. I was expecting her to smile back and tell me her name and something about herself.

'I live here,' I say uncertainly.

Her smile is cool and a little amused as she watches me turn pink. 'I can see that,' is all she says.

I try again. 'Well, my name's Rosalie, and I live here. What's your name?'

She tips her head on one side. 'Don't you already know?'

I feel my cheeks turn pink. 'It's Jasmine, isn't it?'

She raises an eyebrow. 'So, why did you ask?'

My cheeks turn even redder, which seems to amuse her even more. I manage a shrug. 'I was just being polite. Mum says you're the same age as me and you're going to Hanfield High. We'll be in the same year.'

Jasmine looks me slowly up and down. 'I don't think so.'

'You don't think you'll be going to Hanfield High, or you don't think we'll be in the same year?' I ask in confusion.

'I don't think we're the same age,' says Jasmine. 'How old are you – eight ... nine?'

'I'm eleven!' I say indignantly.

She gives a little laugh. It's all tinkly, like tiny bells. 'Seriously, Rosalie – I'm nearly twelve. How old are you?'

I feel my face growing hotter. 'I'm eleven! I'll be twelve in May, and I've finished one term of high school, just like you.'

Jasmine pulls a face. 'If you say so. You're rather small for your age, aren't you?'

She's immediately pointed out the thing I most dislike about myself. I *hate* being the shortest girl in our year. I love netball, but I never made it onto the team in primary school because they only picked the tallest girls. Beth has always played Goal Shooter and she's a fantastic player, but she's a whole head taller than me.

I'm hoping things will be different in high school. Maybe they won't only pick the tall girls, or maybe I'll suddenly grow. I secretly dream of waking one morning to find I've grown 50cm overnight. Mum will take me out to buy new clothes and cool new trainers, and I'll be the tallest on the netball team and shoot all the winning goals.

But it would be stupid to tell Jasmine how much my height bothers me when she clearly didn't mean any harm, so I try again. 'I can introduce you to lots of people. I'll call for you before school each morning and we can walk down together.'

'My goodness, how very kind,' she says.

I look at her more closely. Her words are polite enough, but I'm not too sure about her tone. Perhaps she's a bit shy. She doesn't seem particularly shy, but I know people have different ways of showing it.

Before I can reply, the back door opens, and Mum comes out. She seems pleased to see the pair of us talking together.

'You must be Jasmine,' she says. 'I met your mum yesterday. Welcome to our street.'

Jasmine beams at Mum and walks over to the fence to shake her hand. 'It's *so* nice to meet you, Mrs Watson. I've just been chatting to Rosalie, and she's been *very* kind. It's lovely to know I have a friend already – and a friend in the same year at school too. I'm very lucky.'

'You said you didn't believe we were in the same year,' I say sulkily.

Jasmine laughs her silver bells laugh. 'Oh dear, I seem to have offended you. If so, I can't apologise enough. I simply thought you seemed rather small for twelve. Of course, I'm absolutely delighted to hear you're in my school year. It's *so* wonderful to have a ready-made friend.'

Mum taps my arm. 'Don't be so touchy, Rosalie. You *are* small for your age. You're always grumbling about it, but there's no need to take it out on everyone else. It's very nice to meet you, Jasmine. Do come and visit us whenever you like. We'll always be delighted to see you.'

Jasmine gives Mum a charming smile. 'That is *so* kind, Mrs. Watson. I'll definitely do that. Bye, Rosalie!' She waves and disappears into her house.

'Bye,' I mumble, feeling rather embarrassed by my rudeness. Jasmine probably didn't mean to be unkind when she said I was small, but Mum didn't need to rub it in like that.

'What a *lovely* child,' says Mum, 'and doesn't she have beautiful manners? I hope you two will be good friends.'

'Uh huh,' I say cautiously. I expect Mum's right, and I was just being a bit grumpy. I decide to ask Jasmine over tomorrow so we can get to know each other properly.

Two

When I look out of my bedroom window the next morning, I see Jasmine wandering around her new garden, inspecting the plants. I hesitate for a moment before going outside and walking slowly up her front drive. I'm a little nervous about meeting Jasmine's mum, but maybe she'll ask me to come inside and look around. I love seeing how different people decorate their houses, and I can't wait to see Jasmine's bedroom.

I fix a big smile to my face and ring the doorbell. When nothing happens, I ring again, trying to peer through the frosted glass on the side of the wooden front door. Even though I keep my finger on the buzzer for a long time, there's still no answer, which is really weird. I know Jasmine was home a minute ago because I saw her in the garden.

As I turn to leave, I see Mum walking up the path with Jasmine's mother. Mum looks surprised to see me. 'Rosalie? What are you doing here?'

'I came to see Jasmine,' I say.

'That's nice,' she says. 'This is Jasmine's mother. We met each other at the shops and walked home together. Lynette, this is my daughter, Rosalie. Rosalie, this is ...'

'You may call me Mrs. Robinson,' says Jasmine's mother with a tight smile. 'Hello, Rosalie.'

Jasmine's mum is tall like Jasmine and even more beautifully dressed. Her makeup is perfect, and she looks as though she's come straight from the hairdresser.

'Um … hi,' I say rather awkwardly.

Mrs Robinson looks me up and down for a long moment before turning back to Mum. 'Shall we have that coffee now? Jasmine makes a perfect cappuccino.'

'That sounds lovely,' says Mum.

Before Mrs Robinson can find her key, the door opens, and Jasmine appears. She's wearing a matching skirt and top, and I feel suddenly scruffy in my old jeans and faded T-shirt. Jasmine's blonde hair swishes perfectly across her shoulders as she tips her head on one side, beaming at Mum. 'How very nice to see you again, Mrs Watson.'

I step through the front door behind Mum. 'Hi, Jasmine. You didn't answer the doorbell.'

She jumps slightly, as though she's only just noticed me. 'Rosalie? Where on earth did you spring from?'

I frown. 'I just told you. I was ringing and ringing your bell. Where were you?'

She laughs her bell-like laugh again. 'I suppose I just didn't hear you, which is rather surprising. You do seem quite persistent.'

'Yeah, well, I wondered if you wanted to come over to my house,' I say, feeling rather confused.

'How *very* kind,' she says. 'I only wish I'd heard the bell. As it happens, I'm just about to go out. Another time, perhaps?'

She smiles charmingly at the three of us, and Mum smiles back. I can see exactly what's going through her mind. Jasmine is the perfect child, with the perfect clothes and the perfect manners. Well, that's too bad, I think gloomily. She's stuck with me, and she'll just have to make the best of it.

'Perhaps I could make you a cappuccino before I go,' Jasmine says to Mum. 'My uncle works as a pastry chef in a very nice hotel in Sydney. He's taught me how to make proper coffee as well as how to bake.'

Mum looks delighted as she follows Jasmine inside. I don't think she's even remembered I'm here. I hang around the hall rather awkwardly until Mrs. Robinson notices me.

'Are you still here?' she asks, looking down her nose at me. 'Would you like some juice?'

'Thanks!' I say with enthusiasm. I can't wait to see around the house. Mr. Lambert never let anyone inside.

Jasmine looks surprised when I walk into the kitchen. 'What are you doing here?' she asks.

'Your mum invited me in,' I say.

She spoons two scoops of coffee into a little metal ring. 'Are you sure you didn't misunderstand her? Maybe she said, "Why don't you just go home?"'

I stare at her in shock. 'What do you mean?'

Before Jasmine can answer, Mum opens the kitchen door.

'What a gorgeous house!' she says. 'Are you girls getting to know each other?'

'That's right,' says Jasmine pleasantly. 'I'll just go and let Mum know her coffee's almost ready. Rosalie tells me she's staying for a while. Isn't that lovely?'

'You just said you wanted me to go home!' I blurt out.

Jasmine gives me a puzzled look. 'Excuse me? Oh, I see what you mean.' She turns to Mum. 'I really can't stay after I've made your coffee. I was just explaining to Rosalie that it would be lovely to have her over another time for a nice, long visit.'

'Of course,' says Mum. 'Please don't let us keep you. Rosalie can wait for a time that suits you.'

Jasmine spoons white foam onto the cappuccino, dusts a trail of chocolate powder over the top and hands the cup to Mum. 'I *do* hope you enjoy it.'

She reaches for a tin. 'I made some cupcakes yesterday. Would you like one?'

She pops a pink cupcake onto a small plate and puts it in front of Mum. The cupcake is perfectly iced, with a tiny fondant rosebud on top.

'What can I get for you?' Jasmine asks me. 'I'm *so* sorry, but I'm all out of cupcakes. We have some digestive biscuits, and I could get you a glass of water.'

I shake my head. I could swear I saw several more flashes of pink in the tin before she replaced the lid.

'No, *thank you*,' says Mum. 'Where are your manners, Rosalie? I don't know what you must think of her, Jasmine.'

'I'm sure she didn't mean to be rude, Mrs. Watson,' says Jasmine.

'Don't count on it,' I say under my breath.

'What did you say?' Mum asks suspiciously, but I don't dare repeat it. Jasmine laughs and waves to us both. 'I'm *so* sorry to run away like this, but I have to meet someone.'

She disappears down the hall, and I hear the front door click shut behind her.

Mum sighs. 'How on earth do you expect to make friends with someone like Jasmine when all you do is sulk and shrug and snap at her?'

'I'm not expecting to make friends with her,' I mutter.

She looks surprised. 'Why on earth not? You've been desperate for someone your age to move in next door, but when they do, you turn all sulky and rude. I just don't understand you.'

'She isn't actually that nice,' I say cautiously.

Mum sighs again. 'You're jealous – that's what it is. Jasmine is tidy and polite, and she obviously helps her parents without grumbling. I suppose you think she makes you look bad.'

'She isn't as nice as you think she is,' I say.

I hate this. I can't put my feelings about Jasmine into words. After all, what has she actually done? Perhaps Mum is right, and I'm being suspicious about nothing. Anyway, school starts tomorrow, so Jasmine and I can walk down together. Maybe I'll get to know her a bit better then.

Three

I wake early the next morning and spend a long time staring out of the window, wishing it wasn't the first day of term. I finally push myself out of bed and into the shower. By the time I finish breakfast, I'm feeling a little better.

I leave the house a few minutes earlier than usual so I can call for Jasmine. She must be feeling nervous today. It's always difficult changing schools, and it will be even more difficult for her because the rest of us have been there for a term already.

I run up her front path and ring the bell. There's a long wait before her mother finally appears at the door. When she does, she looks as though there's a bad smell somewhere, but she can't quite place it.

'Oh, it's you again. What can I do for you?' she asks coldly.

'I've come to pick up Jasmine,' I tell her.

'I don't think so,' she says.

I give her my friendliest smile. 'Yes, I have. I said I'd call for her so we could walk down to school together.'

She gives me a frosty look. 'I don't know what you may or may not have told Jasmine, but she left for school a quarter of an hour ago. She likes to arrive in good time for everything, rather than late and out of breath. She's quite right. It doesn't show good manners. Perhaps you should get a move on too?'

She closes the door and I set off down the road by myself, feeling rather crushed. It would have been nice for Jasmine to walk to school with a friend on her first day. I glance at my watch and break into a run. I always plan to leave five minutes early, so I don't have to run the last bit, but I never quite manage it and have to sprint the last hundred metres in order to arrive before the bell. But running is very good for you, so leaving the house late is actually a positive thing. Miss Turner, our PE teacher, is always telling us we should get more daily exercise.

I skid into the classroom two seconds before the bell rings. Beth is already there, and I throw myself into the chair next to her, just as our form tutor walks in.

'Good morning, girls!' she says cheerfully. 'Are you ready for a new term and lots of hard work?'

We all groan, and Miss Chapman laughs. 'Well, you look refreshed and ready to go. Now, we have a new pupil with us today. Where's Jasmine Robinson?'

She looks around the room, and everyone follows her gaze to where Jasmine is sitting two rows behind me with Emma Adams.

Jasmine gives Miss Chapman a huge smile. 'Good morning, Miss Chapman. I'm Jasmine Robinson.'

Miss Chapman smiles back. 'Welcome to Hanfield High. I hope you'll be very happy here.'

Jasmine pushes her long, blonde hair behind her ears. 'Thank you so much. I'm really looking forward to my time here.'

'Oh, vomit!' I whisper to Beth, who looks a bit surprised.

Miss Chapman seems quite impressed by Jasmine's nice appearance and manners.

'Would you like someone to look after you today and make sure you get to all your classes and find your way around the school?' she asks.

A forest of hands shoots up at once. I hesitate for a moment before raising mine too. Jasmine looks around the class, and her eyes rest on me for a long moment before passing on.

'That is *so* kind, Miss Chapman,' she says at last, 'but I think I'll be fine.'

I manage to catch up with Jasmine as we're walking to maths. 'I missed you this morning,' I tell her.

She raises an eyebrow. 'Missed me?'

I feel my face turn pink. 'I went to your house so we could walk down together like we said, remember?'

'No.' She begins to walk faster so I have to jog to keep up.

'Well, we did,' I say. 'Anyway, it doesn't matter. I can call for you tomorrow instead.'

She barely turns her head. 'I leave very early. You won't be ready.'

'I can be ready!' I pant.

She stops and looks down at me with an amused expression. 'I doubt it. I saw you arrive late this morning. Your face was so red, you looked just like a beetroot. Is that why your name is Rosy?' She gives me a small smile and walks off.

I stand in the middle of the corridor, my face flaming. I probably do look like a beetroot, but I can't help it. I always turn red when I'm embarrassed, and even more red when I'm out of breath. Well, that's it! I'm through with trying to help Jasmine Robinson. I'm annoyed to think of all the effort I've already put into her.

When I arrive in the maths room, I sit down next to Beth and pull out my books. Beth gives me a curious look. 'What was all that about? That new girl seems fine.'

I pull a face. 'That's what you think. I'll tell you all about it later.'

Mr. Chase walks in and looks around the room with his usual grumpy expression. 'Stop talking! We have a lot of work to cover this term.'

Everyone hates Mr. Chase. He never says anything nice to anyone. If he truly hates you, he pretends not to know your name, although everyone knows he really does. Last term, he didn't call me by my real name even once.

He spends a while talking about algebra before writing some numbers on the board. 'Take this down in your notebooks!' he barks.

We all start to scribble as quickly as possible, but it's quite difficult because his writing is so awful. I'm just asking Beth whether one of the numbers is a three or an eight when Mr Chase looks over and sees me whispering.

'Didn't I *just* say no talking?' he demands.

'I'm only trying to read your writing, Mr. Chase,' I tell him.

'Rubbish!' he says. 'There's nothing wrong with my writing. You just want an excuse to giggle and whisper with that friend of yours. All right. I'm going to split you up. Beth, you can sit with Emma. Rosa, you can go and sit with … er …'

'My name is Jasmine, sir,' she says politely. 'I'm new here. Of course, Rosalie can come and sit with me. She's welcome to copy off me too. I don't find your writing at all difficult to read.'

Mr Chase gives her an approving nod and I'm surprised to see a half-smile on his face. I didn't think he had any smiling muscles.

'Good,' he says. 'Perhaps you can keep an eye on her and make sure she doesn't talk all the way through my lessons, as she usually does.'

'Of course, sir,' says Jasmine, turning her notebook towards me so I can copy from it. I glare at her, but I can't risk talking again or I'll get a detention. Mr. Chase loves handing those out.

When the bell finally rings, Mr. Chase frowns at us. 'These notes will be needed for your homework, which is on the sheet I gave you. Use the notes to answer the questions. I want your homework handed in first thing tomorrow morning.'

He wipes the board clean then turns and stomps out of the classroom. As soon as he's gone, Jasmine sweeps her notebook into her bag and stands up.

I tap her arm. 'Wait a minute! I'm supposed to be copying your notes, and I haven't finished.'

'That's not my problem,' she says over her shoulder as she walks away.

'I need those notes for my homework!' I call after her, but she's gone.

The rest of the day passes quickly. I manage not to be late for any of my other classes, and I stay as far away from Jasmine as possible. I notice her sitting with Emma and Sara at lunchtime, talking and laughing. She has a stack of tiny, beautifully cut sandwiches in front of her. I quickly hide the lumpy ones I made at top speed this morning because I was worried about being late. I don't want to give her anything else to laugh about.

Beth joins me for lunch, and we eat quickly. They're picking the year seven netball team after school today, and we're both going to try out for it, so Beth wants us to practise this lunchtime. I don't really expect to be picked, but I can't help dreaming about Miss Turner being so impressed with my performance that she congratulates me in front of everyone and gives me the choice of any position I want to play.

Beth will be on the team, of course. She's totally brilliant. One of her feet was turned right in when she was born, but she's had three operations, and they have pretty much fixed it. She can do any sport she likes now, as long as she wears her special orthotic trainers. Even wearing those, she still runs faster than most people I know.

I finish my sandwiches and glance over at Jasmine as she opens her lunchbox and takes out a pink cupcake with a fondant rosebud on top. She catches me staring at her and gives me just the tiniest smile as she takes a bite.

I arrive at the netball court after school in a really bad mood. I'm in the first group, and we all stand on the netball court in the position we want to try out for. I see Miss Turner walking across the grass, and my heart sinks when I see the tall, blonde figure walking beside her.

Jasmine comes over to stand beside me in the middle of the court.

'Are you really trying out for Centre?' she asks. 'At your height? I suppose I ought to congratulate you on your optimism.'

Before I can reply, Miss Turner shouts, 'Toss Up!' and throws the ball high in the air. I'm so angry at what Jasmine has said that I leap for it just a second too late. Jasmine lifts her arms easily and snatches the ball from over my head. She throws it to Wing Attack, and the game begins.

I race after Jasmine, but her long legs make it impossible for me to keep up with her. I'm soon scarlet and sweating, while she stays effortlessly cool. Even her ponytail stays neatly inside its hair tie. Mine has begun to pull free, and I have to push sweaty pieces of hair out of my eyes at crucial moments.

I'm pleased to see Beth shooting goal after goal. I give her a quick thumbs-up, which takes my attention away from the game just long enough for me not to notice the ball flying towards me. The next thing I know, it hits me in the face with a crunching thump, and my eyes are streaming with shock and pain.

Miss Turner runs over to me. 'Are you alright, Rosalie? You really must keep your attention focused on the game.'

Jasmine runs over too, looking concerned. 'Please don't cry, Rosy.'

'I'm not crying!' I snap.

'Oh, I'm so sorry,' she says. 'It's difficult to tell when you're so red. I'm *so* glad you're not badly hurt. Should she sit out for a while, Miss Turner?'

'Good idea,' says Miss Turner. 'Take five minutes on the benches, Rosalie. That was rather a nasty whack.'

'I'm fine,' I say, glaring at Jasmine.

'No, Jasmine is quite right,' she says. 'Off you go.'

I slouch miserably over to the bench, where I sit checking my watch every few seconds. Just as the five minutes is up, Miss Turner blows the final whistle.

'Well played, everyone!' she says. 'Off you go to change now while the next group plays. I'll post the results on the gym noticeboard tomorrow.'

Jasmine jogs past us, looking as cool and fresh as if she's just been for a gentle stroll. She waves at me as she passes. 'Great try-outs! See you in the morning, Rosy.'

Four

I don't call for Jasmine the next morning, although Mum seems to think I should.

'Don't be late, Rosalie,' she tells me at breakfast. 'Jasmine's mum tells me she's always very punctual.'

I shrug. 'Well, she can be punctual all by her stupid self, can't she?'

Mum gives me a sharp look. 'What's eating you today, Miss Grumpy? Did you get out of bed on the wrong side again?'

I've never understood what Mum means by this. My bed is against the wall, and there's only one way to get out of it, which is straight into the pile of clothes I dumped on the floor the previous night. It makes getting dressed in the mornings really easy.

'I called for Jasmine yesterday,' I tell Mum, 'but she didn't even bother to wait or leave a message. She just went without me.'

'Then you should have been a bit earlier, shouldn't you?' she asks. 'That was hardly poor Jasmine's fault.'

Ten minutes later, I'm walking down the road at top speed, stuffing cold toast crusts into my mouth. I'm a little worried about yesterday's maths homework. I forgot to ask Beth for the rest of Mr. Chase's notes, so I had to muddle through the questions as best I could.

I almost went and knocked on Jasmine's door, demanding to see her notes. After all, she did promise Mr. Chase I could copy them. But I was pretty sure her mum would say she wasn't in and would look me up and down as though she'd never in her life seen anyone so scruffy.

I want to get to school before the bell rings so I can catch Beth and compare notes on the last question. I hate maths. I really don't like Mr. Chase, and it doesn't help that our maths classroom overlooks the netball court. I spend most of my lessons watching teams of girls chasing up and down and wishing I was out there with them.

Even though I run most of the way to school, I still only manage to arrive just before the bell. It sometimes feels as though I'm in some weird time zone where, no matter what time I leave home or how fast I run, the bell will be ringing as I arrive. Jasmine of course is in her own special time zone where, no matter how late she leaves home, she'll still arrive early, with her hair neatly brushed and her uniform clean and tidy, and all the teachers will stand in a line and cheer as she walks across the playground.

Our first lesson is maths. It would be. Beth only just arrives in time, so I have no chance to look at her work. Mr. Chase swoops in like a bad-tempered bat and glares around the room.

'Homework, please!' he snaps, waving at Freya to collect our work.

I push my crumpled sheet of paper under Beth's neat one, so no one can see it. With any luck, Mr. Chase might miss it entirely.

'Quiet now, all of you!' he commands. 'Get on with page 74 while I look over your answers. I want to make sure you've all understood yesterday's work.'

He looks up suddenly, like a dog sniffing for a bone, and points at me. 'Rosamund, I thought I told you to sit with Jasmine during maths lessons!'

I stare at him in horror, ignoring the fact that he knows my name perfectly well. He just likes to make me feel small.

'I thought that was only yesterday,' I say.

He squints at me angrily. 'Then you thought wrong, didn't you, Rosemary? I will *not* have people constantly chattering in my classes. Off you go!' He waves a hand at me and goes back to our pile of assignments.

This is so mega unfair! I don't talk during his lessons any more than anyone else, so why is he picking on me? I shove my books into my bag and walk over to where Jasmine is sitting. I bang my books down on her desk.

'You didn't let me finish copying those notes yesterday,' I tell her in an angry whisper. 'How was I meant to do the homework?'

'That's absolutely nothing to do with me.' She flicks her hair and moves her chair slightly away from mine, so I can't see what she's writing.

Mr. Chase looks up and frowns. 'Rhonda, are you *still* talking? What's going on now?'

Jasmine raises her hand. 'Rhonda's upset, sir, because the lesson ended yesterday before she'd copied all my notes. She seems to think I should have been late for my next lesson, just so she could finish.'

'What nonsense!' he says. 'Why should you be late because she isn't organised enough to copy off the board? Roseanne, you are dangerously close to getting a detention.'

I don't answer. If I say anything else, he'll definitely keep me in at lunchtime, and I want to go to the gym with Beth to hear the results of the try-outs.

Mr. Chase buries his head in our assignments again, and I hiss at Jasmine out of the side of my mouth. 'You know perfectly well my name's Rosalie, not Rhonda. I suppose you thought that was funny?'

She claps her hand to her mouth. 'Is that what I said? I'm *so* sorry.' She smiles and turns a page before giving me a sidelong glance. 'But seeing as you ask – yes, I do think you're a bit of a joke.'

Before I can answer, I see Mr. Chase marching towards me, waving a piece of crumpled paper. My heart sinks as I recognise my handwriting.

'Rosalind, what exactly do you mean by this?' he demands, slamming the piece of paper onto the desk in front of me.

I put my arm across the paper, but it's too late. I can tell by Jasmine's delighted smirk that she's seen it too.

Mr Chase is shouting at me now. 'This is beyond a joke, Rachel! You will stay in at lunchtime and re-do the entire thing.'

I don't dare answer, for fear of bursting into tears in front of Jasmine – or hitting her around the head with my school bag.

I spend my lunch hour trying to do the maths problems, even though I still don't understand them. When the bell rings, Mr Chase waves me away without looking up, and I stomp out of the door and make my way to the art room.

Beth is already there, and she gives me a sympathetic look. 'Are you alright?'

I puff out my cheeks. 'Yeah, I suppose. What about the team?'

She doesn't meet my eye, so I know at once I didn't make it.

'Did you get in?' I ask.

She grins, and I hug her. 'That's brilliant! Not that there was any doubt, of course. Are you Goal Shooter?'

She nods. 'I'm really pleased, but it would have been way more fun if you'd got in too.'

'Who got Centre?' I ask suddenly. Centre is my dream position because you get to play all over the court for the entire match.

Beth doesn't answer for a moment, and I suddenly feel as though someone has emptied an entire bucket of ice cubes into my stomach.

'She didn't?' I ask in disbelief.

'I'm afraid so,' says Beth. 'I'm really sorry.'

Just at this moment, Jasmine comes into the classroom. She walks past my desk, bumping into it accidentally-on-purpose. 'Oops! I'm *so* sorry, Rosy. Hi, Beth. Congratulations on making the team. It's all going to be great fun.'

Beth is too annoyed to answer, and Miss Preston arrives before either of us can say anything else.

I go straight home after school. My heart sinks as I walk around the corner and see Jasmine standing at our gate talking to Mum. Just when I thought this day couldn't get any worse!

Mum waits for me to drag my feet up the hill. 'What's all this I hear about your maths homework?' she demands as soon as I join them.

I shoot a poisonous look at Jasmine, who smiles back as sweetly as though she's just given me a birthday present.

'Jasmine has very kindly offered to give you some extra help with your maths this term,' Mum tells me.

I almost choke at this idea. 'She *what?*'

'She's worried about you,' says Mum. 'She's been telling me about your detention. What on earth is going on with you, Rosalie?'

I can't believe what I'm hearing. I glare at them both. 'And has she told you that she wouldn't let me copy her notes, so I couldn't do the assignment?'

'You were being so slow that you were making her late for her next class,' says Mum, and I explode.

'She did it just to be mean and get me into trouble! She's totally horrible. Why can't you see that?'

'So horrible that she's kindly offered to give you some maths tuition in her free time?' asks Mum.

'Over my cold, dead body,' I say.

I can hear by Mum's voice that she's about to lose it. 'You need to grow up, Rosalie!'

Jasmine pulls a fake concerned face. 'Mrs. Watson, please don't be angry with Rosy. I think perhaps she's upset because I got onto the netball team and she didn't.'

'Don't call me Rosy!' I almost shout at her. 'You only do it to annoy me.'

'Oh, I'm *so* sorry,' she says. 'Nothing could have been further from my mind.'

Mum chips in. 'It's hardly Jasmine's fault you didn't make the team, is it? You're being very ungracious about it. How about congratulating her instead?'

'No need, Mrs. Watson,' says Jasmine. 'Don't worry, Rosy. I'm sure you'll grow very soon.'

Mum pats her hand. 'It's very nice of you to take it like that. Congratulations from me, at least.'

'Yeah, congratulations, Jasmine,' I say. 'Congratulations on being the meanest, most spiteful, two-faced …'

Mum cuts me off before I can finish this sentence. 'Stop right there, young lady! I don't know what's wrong with you at the moment. You're bad tempered, you're rude to Jasmine, you aren't doing your homework ...'

'At least I'm not a mean, sneaky little show-off ...' I begin.

Mum interrupts me. 'I forgot. You're one more thing – you're grounded!'

I turn and stomp into the house, leaving Jasmine and Mum gazing after me in silence.

Five

So, now there are two people I'm trying to avoid — Jasmine and Mum. Make that three, actually. I'm also trying to stay well out of Mr. Chase's way. I don't want any more stupid detentions. I want to go to the netball court every lunchtime and practise until I improve so much that Miss Turner *has* to notice me.

Mum and I have another storming row after dinner.

'It isn't me, it's Jasmine!' I yell. 'She's trying to make me look bad.'

Mum gives me an exasperated look. 'Really? She's decided to be neat and tidy and hard-working and helpful, just to show you up?'

'Yes, she has!' I shout, although even I can hear how stupid that sounds.

'I think you're jealous,' says Mum. 'You don't like Jasmine because she's everything you want to be. You want the teachers to like you, but you don't want to put in the work. You want to be taller, so you're picked for the netball team. Well, I can understand that, but there isn't much you can do about it. Instead of concentrating on the things you *can* do something about, you sulk and stamp and behave badly to Jasmine and try to make her look bad too. I'm ashamed to think a daughter of mine could behave like that.'

'I'd be ashamed to have a daughter like her!' I yell. It isn't a particularly good comeback, but it's all I have.

'I think Jasmine's mother is very lucky to have a daughter like her,' she says coldly and walks off.

I'm determined to prove Mum wrong, so I go to bed straight after dinner and set my alarm an hour earlier than usual. It rings uncomfortably early the following morning, but I force myself out of bed and slip out of the house as quickly as possible, determined to get to school before Jasmine. I smile to myself as I picture her face when she walks in to find me sitting in the classroom, cool and tidy and totally organised for the day.

This is such a cheering thought that, in spite of my bad mood, I give a little skip and start to run down the hill. I race around the corner at top speed, not noticing the boy on his bike until it's almost too late. I throw myself into a hedge to avoid him, shrieking in pain as the branches scrape my face and arms.

'Watch out, doofus!' he yells, whizzing off down the road.

I try to pull myself out of the hedge, but I'm stuck in a very spiky part of it. I can feel the blood running down my arms where I've torn my shirt, and my face hurts where the twigs have scratched it.

'Oh, hello, Rosy! I hope you don't mind me mentioning it, but your bag seems to be losing its strap,' says a familiar, sugary sweet voice behind me.

I turn my head with difficulty to see Jasmine pointing towards my backpack, an amused look on her face. The bag has flown into a nearby tree and is hanging upside down from a branch. Most of my textbooks have fallen out, and my papers are fluttering around the garden in the breeze.

'Well, this is a very interesting new look for you,' says Jasmine, her eyes travelling slowly over me, taking in my torn, stained shirt, my bleeding face and the twigs and leaves in my hair.

I stare at her in shock. 'Aren't you going to help me?'

She gives me a puzzled look. 'Help you? Oh, you mean you didn't do this on purpose? It's so hard to tell. You always seem to go in for the crumpled, casual look, so I thought this was just a fashion statement.

'Ha-ha!' I say sulkily. 'Can you get my bag for me while I pick up the papers?'

'Are you serious?' she asks. 'I can't possibly be seen in public with someone who looks like you. I have an image to protect. Bye, then, Rosy. Do try not to be late *again*. You really can't afford to lose more school time. I don't want to tutor you in all our other subjects too.'

'I'll die before I let you tutor me in maths, Jasmine Robinson!' I shout.

'Now, there's a thought.' She smiles and walks away.

I watch her go in shocked silence. Surely, no one could be spiteful enough to walk off without even trying to help their next-door neighbour when they're hanging practically upside down in a hedge? But that's exactly what Jasmine has done. I hate her! I've never hated anyone as much in my entire life. I think about going home and telling Mum what's happened, but she'll have left for work by now, so there's no point. Anyway, I'm still not speaking to her.

I pull myself out of the hedge, tearing my skirt even more, and walk painfully around the garden, picking up all the papers I can find. They're muddy and ripped, and I dread to think what Mr. Chase will say when I hand in last night's homework. I push everything into my bag as best I can. The strap has been almost torn off, so I walk the rest of the way to school cradling it in my arms like a baby. The playground is empty as I walk across to the main entrance and sign in late.

I go to the cloakroom, where I stare at myself in the mirror. My face is covered in mud and dried blood. I wash my face and pull several twigs out of my hair, but I still look pretty awful.

Mr. Chase glances up as I push open the classroom door. 'Ah, Ruby – how good of you to join us! I hope we haven't forced you to hurry at all?'

It's as though he hasn't even noticed something's happened to me.

'Do you have an explanation?' he asks coldly.

I point dramatically to Jasmine, sitting calmly at her desk. 'I had an accident, and *she* didn't even stop to help me.'

'Yes, Jasmine has already told me about it,' he says. 'I gather this so-called accident involved you playing stupid games with a boy on a bike?'

'*What?*' I gasp, hardly able to believe my ears.

He sighs. 'You should have listened to Jasmine when she told you to get to school on time instead of playing tag with your friend and his bike. Sit down, please, Rebecca. You will stay in at lunchtime to catch up. This is becoming quite a regular thing for us, isn't it? Perhaps in time I might even come to look forward to it.'

I bang my way past Beth and Emma and slam my chair into Jasmine's desk. She doesn't even blink. 'You could at least have stopped to wash your face,' she murmurs out of the side of her mouth.

That's it – I quit! I'm never going to get the better of this girl. I'll just have to ask Mum to change my school. At least, I would if I was still speaking to her. Perhaps I'll write her a note.

I don't manage to speak to Beth until the afternoon. She has netball practice at lunchtime, while I'm stuck inside yet again doing algebra with Mr. Chase. I finally get a chance to talk to her while we wait for our history teacher to arrive.

When I tell her what happened this morning, she stares at me in horror. 'I knew she wasn't very nice, but nothing like that! I hope she trips over and breaks her leg on the netball court.'

This is the very worst thing Beth can imagine happening to anyone. She lives for netball, and she'd be absolutely devastated if she ever broke her leg.

I give her a grateful look. 'Thanks, Beth. You couldn't trip her up for me, could you?'

'Probably not,' she says, 'but I'll tell her exactly what I think of her when I see her tomorrow at netball practice. I don't think she'll be quite so pleased with herself when I've finished with her.'

Having even one person on my side makes me feel a bit better. All the teachers think that Jasmine's perfect – even my own mother thinks so. It gives me a warm feeling to know there's someone who believes me. I can't wait to hear what Beth says to Jasmine. She doesn't often get angry, but when she does she can be really scary. Jasmine won't know what's hit her, which totally serves her right.

Six

I stay out of Jasmine's way as much as possible for the rest of the week. When I do see her, she looks as pleased with herself as ever. Beth says she caught her after netball practice and told her what she thought of her, but Jasmine just gave her usual annoying smirk and walked off.

Jasmine manages to say a few nasty things to me over the following few days, but nothing too awful.

I'm surprised she isn't being mean to Beth as well. She can't have enjoyed being told off in public.

I decide in the end that she's probably scared. Beth is twice my size and very good at standing up for herself, which means I'm a much easier target. However, if I stay away from Jasmine and don't remind her that I exist, she may get bored playing games with me.

I'm just happy to get through the rest of the week without any more detentions because there are plenty of other things taking up my time. Our class is having a bake sale on Friday to raise money for our sister school in India, and everyone is really excited.

Beth comes over on Thursday night so we can bake our cakes together. I'm making cupcakes, and she's making chocolate chip cookies. As I open the front door to let her in, I catch sight of a large, blue van pulling away from Jasmine's house. There's a red logo on its side, but I can't make out what it says. I suppose it would be too much to hope it's a moving van.

Beth and I are just taking her last batch of cookies out of the oven when the doorbell rings. Mum goes to answer it and comes back into the kitchen with Jasmine. Beth and I stare at them both in horror, but Jasmine seems absolutely delighted to see us.

'Hi Beth – I didn't know you'd be here!' she says with a friendly smile.

Beth glares back at her, and Jasmine turns to Mum. 'It's our year seven bake sale tomorrow. I've finished all my baking, so I thought I'd come and see whether Rosalie would like a hand with hers.'

Mum looks pleased. 'Isn't that kind, Rosalie?'

I refuse to be forced into pretending to be nice to Jasmine, so I don't even look up from my tray of cupcakes. 'I'm fine,' I say briefly. 'It's all under control.'

'Do you need any help?' Jasmine asks Beth.

'No, I don't,' says Beth shortly, 'so you can just go home again, can't you?'

Jasmine waves a casual hand at us. 'See you tomorrow then, girls. I'm *so* looking forward to tasting your wonderful creations.'

Mum goes with her to the front door. I hear them talking in low voices and Jasmine's tinkling laugh.

When Mum comes back into the kitchen, her face is pink with anger. 'I've just about had it with you and your rudeness, Rosalie, and I'd certainly have expected better of you, Beth! Don't tell me you've taken against poor Jasmine too?'

Beth looks horribly embarrassed, but she doesn't let me down. 'Actually, Mrs Watson, she's really nasty. She's very mean to Rosalie at school. It's only the teachers who can't see it.'

Mum's voice becomes even colder. 'So Rosalie tells me, but I'm surprised she's managed to convince you too. It's very unpleasant to see girls of your age behaving like three-year-olds fighting at pre-school. Now, if that last batch of cookies is ready, I think it's time you were going home, don't you?'

I walk to the door with Beth, lowering my voice so Mum can't hear. 'That really wasn't your fault.'

Beth doesn't seem too bothered. 'Don't worry about it. See you tomorrow.'

I stick my chin in the air as I walk past Mum, and she doesn't even try to speak to me.

We still aren't speaking to each other the following morning. I leave the house and walk slowly down the hill with my box of cupcakes. I peer around the corner in case that stupid boy is there with his bike, but I can't see anyone. I'm so relieved that I don't even hear the footsteps behind me until something bangs my elbow. The box of cakes flies out of my hands, most of them landing upside down on the grass.

'Oops, *so* sorry about that, Rosy! You're so small I didn't see you,' says Jasmine's voice as she walks past me and on to school.

I bend down and turn the box over. The cakes aren't completely broken, but they're pretty battered, and there's icing everywhere. I tidy them up as best I can and follow Jasmine at a safe distance, wondering why she isn't carrying anything.

When we go to the hall to set up our tables, I see Jasmine's mother standing near the door, holding several large boxes. I slip past her without speaking and join Beth, who's busy laying out her cookies on a white plate.

I open my box, and she stares at the cupcakes in horror. 'What on earth happened? Oh, don't tell me!'

I nod silently. It doesn't seem worth saying anything else. We arrange the cakes as best we can and eat the broken bits. They still taste pretty good, so maybe people will look past their appearance and buy them anyway.

As soon as the bell rings for morning break, the doors fly open and it's total chaos. Two hundred girls rush into the hall, looking excitedly up and down the tables. There's the noise of coins clinking into bowls and everyone talking loudly through mouthfuls of cake. Most people seem to have gathered at the far end of the hall, and only one girl comes over to buy one of Beth's cookies.

'What's going on down there?' asks Beth as she hands back the change.

The girl points towards the longest table. 'It's that new girl, the one with the blonde hair. She's selling the most amazing cakes. She made them all herself. She must be a brilliant cook. Go and take a look.' She gives a quick glance at my battered cupcakes and walks off.

Beth and I abandon our cakes and walk as quietly as we can to Jasmine's table. The girl was right. These cakes do look pretty amazing. There's a silver stand entirely covered in cupcakes, all beautifully decorated with swirls of rainbow icing, sprinkles and silver balls. There are buns with chocolate shapes piped onto the buttercream and a huge plate of éclairs filled with fresh cream. There are fat, sugary doughnuts oozing with jam and huge cream slices swirled with vanilla and caramel icing. Hands are appearing from everywhere to grab the cakes, and the box next to Jasmine is stuffed with notes and coins.

'I do like to make my own puff pastry,' I hear Jasmine's smug voice saying to Miss Turner. 'It isn't really difficult when you've been baking as long as I have. I always think it tastes so much better than shop bought pastry.'

'I'd certainly agree with that,' says Miss Turner. 'Those cupcakes are absolutely beautiful, Jasmine. I really think you could charge a little more for them.'

She scribbles a new price tag and props it next to the last of the cupcakes before pointing to some delicious looking biscuits, beautifully piped and crisp and golden. 'And what are these?'

'They're *langues de chat*,' says Jasmine, looking even more pleased with herself than usual. 'It's French, and it means *cats' tongues*.'

Beth snorts loudly and leans over Jasmine's shoulder to look at the cakes. 'Cats' tongues, Jasmine? Can I have a lick?'

Miss Turner shakes her head at the pair of us. 'Don't be so childish, girls! Why aren't you two still at your table? Have you sold out?'

'I almost forgot!' says Jasmine. 'I promised Rosalie I'd buy one of her delicious cakes. Could you possibly watch my table for a moment, Miss Turner?'

'Of course,' says Miss Turner.

Jasmine follows us down the hall. For one desperate moment, I wonder whether to pretend one of the other tables is ours, but it's no good. She heads straight for my cakes and looks at the price tag in mock horror. '*Cupcakes – one dollar.* A whole dollar, Rosy? You aren't serious, are you?'

'Maybe they'd look a bit better if you hadn't knocked them onto the grass,' says Beth loyally.

Jasmine looks at the cakes again. 'I really doubt it. Here you are, Rosy. Here's what they're worth.' She hands me a five-cent coin and walks away.

By the end of breaktime, most of Beth's cookies have sold, but my cakes stay where they are until I reduce them to 20 cents and a few of them finally sell. When the bell rings we all gather around Miss Turner, who's looking absolutely delighted.

'This has been our best cake sale ever!' she says. 'Our sister school will be very pleased. Have you added up all your takings?'

Everyone hands her their money. Beth's flapjacks have made twenty dollars, and most other people have made about the same. My cakes have made one dollar twenty, and I put the money in the box very quickly, hoping Jasmine won't notice. She does, of course. I see her eyes fixed on me as I drop the silver coins into the pot.

Jasmine is the last to put her money in. She has so many notes and coins that it takes her quite a few minutes to count them. She straightens up at last with a modest smile. 'Three hundred and forty dollars.'

Miss Turner beams at her. 'That's absolutely wonderful! It will pay for several new desks. Let's have a round of applause for Jasmine and all her hard work.'

Everyone claps, except for me and Beth. Jasmine leans towards me under cover of the applause and whispers, 'Never mind, Rosy. You did awfully well too. I should think your yummy cupcakes have made enough money to buy ... let me see ... a pencil?'

She turns away before I can answer, leaving me determined to get my revenge on her, if it's the last thing I do.

Seven

Beth comes over on Friday afternoon after netball practice. I really wanted to stay and watch so we could walk home together, but I'm keeping away from the netball courts whenever Jasmine's there. This means I'm seeing Beth far less often, which feels horribly unfair.

We make ourselves enormous ice cream sodas and carry them out to the garden, although not until

I've taken a quick look over the fence to make sure Jasmine isn't around. As we drink, Beth tells me that Roper Girls High School has challenged our netball team to a match in the last week of term. Roper Girls High is a really posh school on the other side of town. They have a new netball coach who's very friendly with Miss Turner, and the pair of them have agreed to a challenge match.

Beth is hugely excited about the game. 'Roper Girls High wins absolutely everything!' she tells me. 'We've never beaten them at netball or swimming, and I know how much it would mean to Miss Turner if we could do it this time.'

'I like Miss Turner,' I say thoughtfully. 'She's really fair. I wish I was on the team, but even I can see that Jasmine's better than me.'

Beth is too honest to pretend. 'She *is* good. She has long legs, and she's very fit, but I hate her being on the team. She says mean things to everyone before practice starts, but as soon as Miss Turner arrives she's really lovely.'

'What about you?' I ask. 'Is Jasmine mean to you?'

Beth laughs. 'She stays well clear of me, but I've seen her looking sideways at me once or twice. She's like a vampire – I wouldn't want to meet her on a dark night.'

We collapse into giggles and are still snickering into our sodas when a familiar voice reaches us. 'Good evening, girls! Having a good laugh about Rosy's latest maths homework?'

Jasmine must have come outside while we were talking, and I wonder how much she heard. We weren't exactly talking quietly.

'Shut up, Jasmine!' Beth calls back. 'There's no one here to admire you right now.'

'Are you absolutely sure?' asks Jasmine, and my heart sinks as I see Mum opening our back door.

Jasmine must have seen her through our kitchen window.

'Everything all right, girls?' asks Mum.

Beth and I nod but don't speak.

'Good evening, Mrs. Watson. How are you?' calls Jasmine.

Mum gives her a friendly wave. 'Hello, Jasmine. I didn't see you there. How's school?' I'm sure I don't imagine the quick look she shoots me.

'School is absolutely wonderful, thank you,' says Jasmine. 'Everyone is *so* friendly and helpful.'

'Well, that's good to hear,' says Mum rather doubtfully.

'Have you heard about the netball challenge match?' asks Jasmine. 'It's against Roper Girls High, and all the year seven parents are invited. It's going to be *such* fun.'

She gives me a quick look before clapping her hand to her mouth. 'Oh, I'm *so* sorry, Rosy! I forgot.'

'Don't be silly,' says Mum. 'It all sounds very exciting. We'll be there to cheer you on, won't we, Rosalie?'

'I suppose so,' I mutter.

'Are you coming over?' Mum asks Jasmine. 'We have ice cream sodas.'

Jasmine pretends to look anxiously at me and Beth before shaking her head. 'That is *so* kind, Mrs Watson, but Rosalie and Beth probably think it would be nicer if it was just the two of them.' She gives her fake laugh and waves goodnight.

'Too right, it would!' I burst out as soon as she disappears, forgetting that Mum's still here.

She gives us both a long look. 'Would it have been so very difficult to be welcoming and gracious?'

She goes back into the house, shutting the door firmly behind her.

'Too right, it would!' repeats Beth, looking over at Jasmine's garden. 'I bet she was just waiting there in the shadows for your mum to come out. She's like a giant, blonde ... spider.'

And we start giggling again.

I try to forget about Jasmine over the next couple of weeks. We're getting much more homework this term, and I don't want any more bad grades. If I don't do well, Jasmine will immediately find a way to let Mum know, and she'll offer to tutor me – torture me, more like.

I go down to the netball court with Beth as often as possible, and we spend hours practising passing and catching and shooting goals. I hardly ever get the ball into the basket, but Beth makes me practise jumping as high as I can until I'm exhausted. She says it's good training for when I make the team. She drops ball after ball neatly into the net, and I tell her she's going to be fine.

'But what if I'm not?' she asks. 'I keep having nightmares where I drop every single ball and

Jasmine runs up and catches them and scores lots of goals.'

'She couldn't, even if she wanted to,' I say. 'Centre isn't allowed in the goal circle. It's in the rules.'

Beth shrugs. 'I know, but she'd probably manage to get the rules changed, just for that match.' She puts on a sickly Jasmine voice. 'Ooh, Miss Turner, I really *love* your new hairstyle! Have you lost weight recently? By the way, could you *possibly* change the entire rules of netball just for me? Oh, you could? That is just *so* kind.'

I'm choking with laughter now. 'You know it would never happen.'

'I'm not so sure,' says Beth gloomily.

'She's such a loser,' I say, and we look around us guiltily, half-expecting Jasmine to pop up from behind a bush.

I give Beth's arm a comforting pat. 'All you have to do is concentrate on not breaking your arms or legs before the match.'

'You really think Jasmine would go that far?' she asks. 'You're probably right.'

The match is taking place after school on Tuesday, and it looks as though the whole of our year group will be there to cheer on the team. Even Mum is finishing work early to come and watch. At any other time, I'd think that was really nice of her, but not today. All I can think about is Jasmine racing up and down the court with her perfect blonde ponytail and her perfectly ironed netball kit and her perfectly modest smile each time someone claps for her. Still, there's nothing I can do about that. I'm going to the match to cheer for Beth and the other members of the team, not Jasmine.

As soon as our last lesson finishes on Tuesday afternoon, we run around to the netball courts. The Roper team has already arrived and is doing a series of complicated warm-up drills. They've even brought their cheerleaders with them. People are starting to point and giggle, but the team doesn't seem to notice, and neither do the cheerleaders.

They begin to run around the edge of the court in formation, waving letters spelling out ROPER. They're also doing some really impressive back flips.

I imagine myself kicking my legs really high when our team comes out, yelling, 'Give me a B, give me an E, give me a T ...' Beth would *die* of embarrassment.

I try again. 'Don't give me a J, don't give me an A ...'

But my stupid imaginings come to a sudden stop when I see our team standing together on the grass a little way away. They're all gathered around Beth, and even at this distance I can see the tears pouring down her face.

Eight

I drop my bag on the grass and race over to the group of girls. 'What's going on, Beth? Are you ill?'

She shakes her head. I can hardly hear what she's saying through her storm of sobs, but I just manage to make out two words – *'Trainers'* and *'Disappeared.'*

I laugh in relief. 'Is that all? I thought you must have broken your arm or something. You can't find your trainers? I can go and look for them, if you like, or you can borrow someone else's.'

'No, I can't!' she sobs. 'They're my orthotic trainers.'

I'd forgotten about that. I stare at her helplessly. 'Couldn't you borrow another pair, just for this match?'

She looks at me as though I've gone mad. 'After three operations? My mum would kill me. She'd never let me risk it. No – someone else will just have to play instead.'

I can see it almost destroys her to say this. Miss Turner comes running out of the building and puts her arm around Beth. 'No luck?' she asks.

Beth wipes her eyes. 'Not yet. I'm sorry to be such a wuss.'

Miss Turner gives her a hug. 'Don't be so silly. It's a huge disappointment.'

Jasmine steps forward and puts an arm around Beth's other shoulder. 'You poor, poor thing. This must be awful for you. I'm so, *so* sorry.'

Beth shakes her off. 'Yeah, right!'

Miss Turner looks startled. 'Beth, that's enough! I know how disappointed you must be, but Jasmine is speaking for the entire team.'

'Whatever!' snaps Beth, sitting down on the grass and wiping her eyes.

I notice Mum standing nearby with Jasmine's mother, both of them looking quite shocked at Beth's behaviour. I look at Jasmine, and I know I'm not imagining it. Underneath that fake concerned expression is a faint smile, and I suddenly know exactly what must have happened. This is Jasmine's revenge on Beth for shouting at her in front of everyone. I'm absolutely sure of it, but I'm not sure I'll be able to prove it in time.

I turn and race upstairs to the changing rooms as fast as I can. Jasmine's best friend Emma is standing next to her locker and looks startled to see me. I make a grab for her locker handle, but she's already turned the key.

'Open it right now!' I order, but she just gives an annoying smirk and turns away. I grab her arm. 'Do it now, Emma, or I'll ...'

I trail off. I don't know exactly what I'll do, but I'm definitely not letting Emma and Jasmine get away with this.

'You'll what?' she teases me.

'I'll go and get Miss Turner,' I say.

Emma just laughs. 'But it's my *private* locker. She can't make me open it, and certainly not in time for the match. My key's been stolen from my school bag, you see, so I couldn't open it even if I wanted to. If Miss Turner manages to get a new key and open it later, I simply won't have *any* idea who could have stolen my key and put those shoes in there. It might have been anyone. It might even have been the girl who's jealous that her best friend got picked for the team and that she didn't because she's such a midget.'

She holds out the locker key teasingly and I make a grab for it. She laughs again. 'You'll have to be a lot quicker than that.'

She raises her arm high in the air. I jump at it several times, but, like every other person in my year, Emma is a lot taller than me.

'You're just like my pet spaniel,' she says mockingly. 'Come on, girl – fetch!'

I jump again, and this time she isn't so lucky. As she lifts her arm out of my reach, the key slips from her hand and flies high into the air. I see the horror on her face as she realises what's happened. Everything seems to go into slow motion, just like a movie, and it feels as though I have forever to prepare myself. This is where all my netball practise with Beth is going to pay off.

As the key begins to fall, I summon up every bit of energy I have and try to remember everything

Beth has taught me. Emma and I both leap together, but it's my hand that touches the key first, my fingers that close tightly around it.

Emma gives a scream of pure rage. 'Give that back right now! It's mine!'

She claws at my face, but I don't care. I leap across to her locker and ram the key into the lock. The door swings open, and I snatch up Beth's trainers and disappear down the stairs with Emma yelling after me, 'My father's a lawyer. We're going to sue you!'

I just laugh and keep going. I run across the grass and drop the trainers in front of Beth, who gives a shriek of disbelief and jumps to her feet. 'Miss Turner, she's found them! She's found them!'

Everyone comes running, and I glance over at Jasmine. She sees me looking at her and quickly turns her look of horror into a look of delight, but it's too late. If I had any doubts before, I certainly don't have any now.

'Would you like to know who stole these?' I ask Miss Turner as calmly as possible.

She spins around to face me. '*What?*'

'It was her!' I point firmly at Jasmine, no longer caring what she might say. I'm not letting her wriggle out of this one.

Jasmine's mother rushes forward, her face scarlet with rage. 'How *dare* you say such a thing about my daughter?'

I ignore her. 'You *have* to believe me, Miss Turner. You just *have* to.'

Miss Turner stares into my anxious face. 'That's a very serious accusation, Rosalie. Can you back it up?'

I nod. 'As soon as I heard Beth's trainers had been stolen, I knew who must have done it …'

Jasmine breaks in. 'I'm not listening to any more of this! I know you hate me, Rosalie, although I've never known exactly why. But I didn't know you hated me quite this much.' She buries her face in her hands and gives a fake sob.

I roll my eyes and carry on. 'I went upstairs to check the lockers because that was the obvious hiding place.'

Jasmine looks up quickly. Just as I suspected, there are no tears on her face.

'Miss Turner, this is ridiculous!' she says. 'I haven't been anywhere near Emma's locker today. You can ask her yourself.'

My mouth falls open in shock. This is unbelievable. I turn very slowly to face Jasmine. 'Who said the trainers were in Emma's locker?'

A horrified look comes over Jasmine's face as she realises what she's just said. 'You did ... you, er ... you said to Miss Turner ...'

I shake my head, watching the expressions of the adults around us slowly change. It's absolutely magical.

'No,' I say very calmly. 'The only person who mentioned Emma's locker was you. It's amazing, though, because that's exactly where I did find them. Can you explain that?'

This is brilliant. Jasmine is slowly turning as red as I always do, but her redness isn't embarrassment – it's sheer rage. She looks around at all the people staring at her in horror, for once not taking her side, not believing her, and suddenly she loses it.

She jabs her finger at me. 'You're all going to listen to ... to ... *her*? She's so stupid that she can't even copy her maths homework off the board without a babysitter. She can't catch a ball, but she thought she could try out against *me* for Centre.'

She turns quickly and points at Beth. 'And you! How *dared* you tell me off in front of everyone? Who do you think you are, you total loser? Yes, I hid your stupid orthotic shoes. You deserved to lose them. That'll teach you to speak to me like that!'

She bursts into tears of rage, and her mother runs over to hug her, glaring around at the other parents.

'What are you all looking at?' she demands. 'You're just jealous because Jasmine is prettier and smarter and better at sport than any of your daughters. Do any of you know who we are? My brother is a *top* pastry chef in Sydney. He wins awards for his work. He made hundreds of cakes for your stupid bake sale. Do you have any idea how much money we raised for you?'

Jasmine waves frantically at her mother to shut her up, and I see Miss Turner's face go pink as she remembers the cakes. Jasmine's mother starts to walk away from us, still holding Jasmine's hand. When she reaches the path, she turns and stares back at us.

'You're jealous! You're all just jealous – especially you!' She points her finger at me, and I wink back cheerfully.

Miss Turner steps forward, looking shaken. 'I think it's time we put an end to this. We have a guest team with us today, and I won't have another school thinking this sort of behaviour is normal for us. Rosalie, did you say you found Beth's shoes in Emma's locker?'

I throw her the locker key, and she stares at it. 'Where on earth did you get this?'

I think about this for a moment. 'Toss Up, Miss Turner.'

She raises an eyebrow. 'That must have been quite some jump. Well, as Jasmine is no longer on the team, I think you should play Centre for us today. Can you be changed and onto the court in two minutes?'

I head for the changing rooms at top speed, hearing Jasmine's howl of rage as I go. I'm back downstairs in less than two minutes and see Mum walking towards me holding a bib marked C. She looks really upset as she helps me tie it on.

'I'm so sorry, love,' she says in a low voice.

I stare at her until she looks me in the eyes. 'Do you still think Jasmine's mother is lucky to have a daughter like her?'

Mum lifts her hands. 'You win. I've never seen anything quite like it. I didn't think someone like Jasmine would be capable of that sort of behaviour.'

I give her an innocent look. 'But she's so neat and tidy and hard-working and helpful.'

She hugs me. 'I'm very glad to have the daughter I have. Will that do for now?'

I hug her back and run onto the court, my heart nearly bursting with excitement.

I wish I could say I dazzle everyone with my brilliance, but I don't. In fact, I hardly manage to get the ball at all, but I try my absolute best. When the match ends, I look like a sweating beetroot, as Jasmine would say, but for once I don't care.

Miss Turner claps me on the back. 'Well done, Rosalie! You put your heart and soul into that. I'm going to make you our official team reserve. Would you like to come along to team training on Thursday?'

I give her a huge grin. 'I'd love to! Thanks, Miss T.'

I walk back to the changing rooms with the rest of the team, all of us chattering and laughing. Yes, we lost by a landslide, but no one really seems to care. It's only a game, after all. Anyway, something tells me it won't be me who gets the blame for us losing yet again to Roper Girls High.

The Principal's door is slightly open when we walk past, and I glance inside to see Jasmine, Emma and both their mothers standing silently in front of the desk. The Principal looks absolutely furious.

Beth winks at me and puts on her Jasmine voice. 'I'm just so, *so* sorry. It really couldn't have happened to a nicer person.'

We double over with laughter before heading towards the changing rooms as quickly as possible.

There's an afternoon tea waiting for us in the hall, and they always give us doughnuts when there's a visiting team. If we're really, *really* lucky, there might even be cats' tongues.

Thank you for reading this book. I do hope you enjoyed it. If you did, please consider leaving a review on Amazon. It helps new readers find my books, and I really appreciate it.

Also, please visit my website at rjwhittaker.com for news about upcoming books, free offers and competitions. If you have questions about Pom Pom or any of my other books, you can contact me directly via the website. I always love talking to readers and hearing their thoughts and suggestions.

About the Author

RJ Whittaker was born in the UK, but she got lost one day and now lives a few miles away in Australia. She learned to read long before you did, so you probably have some catching up to do. If you like books as much as she does, you'll probably enjoy reading about a monkey called *Pom Pom*. He came to live with RJ's family several years ago and has caused so much trouble that RJ often thinks about running away to get some peace.

If monkeys aren't your thing – although they really should be – you'll probably enjoy RJ's books about people just like you. There's *Hannah Takes The Lead* – a story about a girl who lands her dream part in the school play but loses all her friends, and *Jasmine Moves In* – a story of bullying, cupcakes and sweet revenge.

To find out more about these books, and maybe even win yourself a free copy, just follow the trail of banana skins to my website at www.rjwhittaker.com.

Also by R J Whittaker

Hannah Takes The Lead

She's always wanted to be a star – she just didn't realise it would be so complicated!

Hannah can hardly believe her luck when she lands the lead role in the school play. Her dream of being a famous actor is finally coming true!

Her best friend Ashleigh seems less excited, but that's her problem. Hannah is soon too busy to think about anything except the play – and the understudy she suspects is trying to sabotage her.

But as the performance draws near and the pressure grows, Hannah begins to wonder whether achieving her ambition was worth losing her best friend.

For everyone who's ever dreamed of being an actor – a fast-paced, amusing story of drama, sabotage and friendship – of discovering your true self and what really matters.

Pom Pom The Great

A boy who needs a friend and a monkey who needs a home ...

When Pom Pom leaps through the bedroom window one night, he turns James' life upside down. Pom Pom tells everyone he's the tidiest, quietest, most helpful monkey anyone has ever met, and the family is lucky to have him.

There's just one small problem. James refuses to get rid of his badly behaved teddy bear, who quickly becomes Pom Pom's worst enemy. One of them has to go, and Pom Pom is determined it won't be him.

If James wants Pom Pom to stay, he has to promise to keep him out of trouble. What could possibly go wrong?

Pom Pom Moves House

Pom Pom's family is on the move, and there's plenty to do. It's lucky he's such a helpful monkey, always willing to lend a paw. The family would never get through it all without him. Pom Poms are the very best at moving house.

Pom Pom Starts School

School quickly becomes one of Pom Pom's very most favourite things. He can hardly wait to show his school report to Teddy. If that doesn't prove which one of them is the smartest, nothing will. Pom Poms are the very best at going to school.

Pom Pom The Pirate

After a successful term at school, it's time for Pom Pom's first summer holiday. He swims in the sea, disguises himself as an iceberg, battles a giant crab and discovers a treasure map. Pom Poms are the very best at summer holidays.

Pom Pom The Brave

When Pom Pom needs to have his tonsils out, he knows how much his family will miss him. He must get home as quickly as possible to look after them. Luckily, Pom Poms are the very best at having operations.

Pom Pom Helps Out

Mum's sister is having a baby, and Pom Pom and Mum go to Scotland to help out. While he's there, Pom Pom visits a castle, hunts for ghosts and tries to steal the crown jewels. He's also happy to help out when his new cousin arrives. Pom Poms are the very best at babies.

Made in the USA
Las Vegas, NV
24 November 2021